Menopause Naturally

A wide range of natural
therapies to help
women through this
challenging passage

Carolyn Dean, M.D.

Keats Publishing, Inc.  New Canaan, Connecticut

ABOUT THE AUTHOR

Carolyn Dean received her M.D. from Dalhousie University in Halifax, Nova Scotia, Canada. She had a private practice in nutritional medicine in Toronto for 12 years, incorporating herbs, homeopathy, acupuncture and nutrition. Dr. Dean now lives in New York where she does clinical research in homeopathic acupuncture. She is the author of *Complementary Natural Prescriptions for Common Ailments* and *Homeopathic Remedies for Common Children's Ailments*, both published by Keats Publishing, Inc.

Menopause Naturally is not intended as medical advice. Its intent is solely informational and educational. Please consult a health professional should the need for one be indicated.

MENOPAUSE NATURALLY

ISBN: 0-87983-681-4

Printed in the United States of America

Good Health Guides are published by
Keats Publishing, Inc.
27 Pine Street (Box 876)
New Canaan, Connecticut 06840-0876

Contents

INTRODUCTION

Life is a series of natural and spontaneous changes.
Don't resist them—that only creates sorrow.
Let reality be reality.
Let things flow naturally forward in whatever way they like.
LAO-TSE

As more and more women are taking charge of their bodies they are looking for natural treatments for the symptoms of menopause.

My own approach to the empowering transition of menopause is based on the following beliefs:

• Menopausal symptoms are lessened in women who have a healthy diet, exercise regularly and have a healthy outlook on life.

• Hypoglycemic symptoms are exacerbated by menopause and should be treated with a proper eating schedule and a low refined carbohydrate diet.

• There are dozens of natural remedies for menopause and the symptoms of menopause.

• Hormone Replacement Therapy (HRT) may be necessary for some women; in this case natural hormones can be used instead of synthetic ones.

• Each woman must study the options, take responsibility for her own health and make her own decision on menopausal therapy. Then she must find a doctor who will work with her.

With menopause, which occurs between the ages of 45 and 55, the ovaries naturally slow down and cease their production of estrogen and the monthly menstrual flow stops. At this time the adrenal glands become a major source of post-menopausal estrogen. While menopause is a natural biological occurrence, unnatural circumstances, such as adrenal stress, accumulation of infectious organisms and the overuse of drugs, can make it a more difficult time.

These unnatural circumstances also include the barrage of advertising that forces women to make the impossible choice between taking synthetic hormones (which include a risk of breast cancer) or not taking synthetic hormones (which they are told increases the risk for heart disease or osteoporosis). Thus menopause, the time for a woman now released from the burden of childbearing and child rearing to grow spiritually and intellectually and take her place as a "wise woman" in the community, instead becomes a time of unnecessary fear and confusion.

Stress, which leads to overactive and then depleted adrenal glands, causes symptoms of anxiety, panic attacks and hypoglycemia. During menopause, as the ovaries put out less and less estrogen, the adrenals take over to secrete more sex hormones than before. However, if the adrenals are depleted by stress, sugar, caffeine or alcohol, they fail in this important function. Natural therapies must aim at restoring these important organs and their functions.

MENOPAUSAL DETOXIFICATION

Statistically, women are healthier than men up to the age of menopause. Menstrual periods flush toxins from the body along with the accumulated blood in the uterus. The mere retention of these toxins, when the period stops, may cause some of the symptoms of menopause and make us more susceptible to illness at the same rate as men. Also, as we age, the organs of elimination may not work as efficiently.

Therefore, at menopause, women should begin a regular regime of cleansing to take the place of their periods.

Medicine traditionally ignores the importance of both proper absorption of nutrients and elimination of body toxicity in dealing with illness; however, it is essential to recognize that proper digestion and absorption, elimination, skin cleansing and detoxification are crucial to good health and to healing.

As you change your diet and lifestyle, you go through a detoxification process that may include withdrawal headaches as you first eliminate coffee, alcohol and cigarettes. You may also aggravate symptoms if you try to go back to them.

In other words, once the body is able to feel better, if toxic substances are ingested the body may have a severe reaction to them, and immediate feedback should warn you to avoid these substances. This is in fact a good sign; this is the way the body encourages you to avoid ingesting anything harmful to your health.

Many menopausal women complain of joint aches and pains, arthritis and rheumatism. If it is correct that toxins that are no longer eliminated at the monthly period are building up in the body, then the treatment is fairly straightforward. Cleanse the body and don't add more drugs to the toxic load you already carry.

The symptoms of intestinal toxemia include fatigue, nervousness, gastrointestinal discomfort, impaired nutrition, skin eruptions, headaches, endocrine disturbances, neurocirculatory abnormalities, arthritis, sciatica, low back pain; allergy, asthma, eye, ear, nose and throat disease; cardiac irregularities and changes in the breasts. All these conditions have responded to natural therapies that can reverse the toxemic state in the intestines. Yet many of these conditions are considered manifestations of menopause.

Medications, particularly antidepressants, codeine, and antacids containing aluminum are yet another cause of toxemia. It is advisable to avoid these medications, but if you must take them, drink at least eight glasses of water per day.

Between one and three bowel movements a day is a normal pattern; however, our fiber-poor diet makes us so sluggish that a bowel movement only every three to four days is considered normal! This is a very dangerous belief. The longer discarded or undigested food products remain in the large intestine, the more they putrefy. This putrefaction creates harmful waste products which can be reabsorbed into the blood stream, and some of these poisons may be carcinogenic. The headache which is characteristic of constipation is caused by poisonous products and the irritation they cause.

Treatment for Constipation:
- Bran fiber: wheat, oat or rice bran. The dosage is one to three tablespoons in cereal or mixed in juice daily plus an extra glass or two of water.
- A diet rich in vegetables, whole grains, nuts and seeds.
- Psyllium seed powder or capsules. The dosage is one teaspoon shaken in eight ounces of water followed by an additional eight ounces of water. Start with once a day and then go to twice a day if needed. A little juice can be added for taste. If you use psyllium without extra water you can actually cause constipation. Psyllium should not be taken with meals to prevent nutrients from being absorbed in the bulk and removed from the body. First thing in the morning and last thing at night is best.
- Two extra glasses of water alone can increase bowel movements. Eight glasses of water a day are optimal. Drink six ounces at a time and don't drink water with meals.
- Castor oil packs. Place on the abdomen to help stimulate lymphatic circulation of the bowel.
- Massage. Massage of the large intestine is done by massaging upwards on the abdomen on the right side, across the top of the abdomen just above the umbilicus and downward on the left side of the abdomen.
- Exercise. This helps to speed up bowel transit time and encourage detoxification.
- Fasting. This is another cleansing technique. Strict water fasting is rarely recommended. With the burden of toxins we carry, a strict detoxification action is too overwhelming to the organs of elimination.

After a regimen of good diet, exercise and sufficient sleep has been implemented and maintained for a minimum of one month you can begin one-day fasts each week on vegetable broths and vegetable juices. Use psyllium seed powder or capsules to increase the bowel movements while on the fast. You must, of course, consult with your doctor before doing this since your particular condition might not lend itself to fasting of any sort. Particularly useful in the detoxification process are:

- Broths and/or juices made from celery, carrots, potatoes, kale, turnips, parsnips, etc. Avoid using broccoli and brussels sprouts. Because of their high sulphur content, the broth would be too strong. Juice fasting can be done for a three-day period every two to three months. This gives the body a good rest from digestion, and toxins which are held in fat storage have a chance to be eliminated.

- Aloe vera gel for healing the intestines and for detoxification; take one tablespoon in juice every morning.

Candidiasis

Candida albicans is a one-celled yeast or fungus which lives in the gastrointestinal tract. Under the influence of antibiotics, the birth control pill, cortisone, a highly refined bread and sugar diet, that glass of wine every night at dinner, and/or stress, yeast begin to overgrow. Their toxins and byproducts can adversely affect the whole body. In menopause the use of synthetic estrogens can cause yeast overgrowth. Also, the fragility of vaginal tissue can lead to infections, more use of antibiotics and more *candida* overgrowth.

The symptoms are numerous and may include headaches, head congestion, depression and anxiety, throat and chronic cold symptoms, swollen glands, coated tongue, gastric upset, gas and bloating, constipation or diarrhea, vaginitis, arthritis, cystitis, muscle and joint aches and numbness and tingling of the extremities.

The best way to diagnose this condition is through special culture and anti-fungal drug-sensitivity testing and blood antibody tests. With these scientific tests, doctors are able to diagnose and treat each person individually.

The treatment usually begins with a very strict diet which eliminates sugar, bread with yeast, fruit, fermented foods, and often most grains for a few weeks. Most women with *candidiasis* report that they begin to feel much better by the second or third week. The first week may be uncomfortable, with an aggravation of symptoms as the yeast dies off, flooding the system, even causing more symptoms than before. After several weeks on a strict diet, a reintroduction of foods (one at a time) would indicate whether that food is one of the culprits—either a food allergy or a yeast-promoting food. Sometimes it is necessary to have food allergy testing done to determine specific allergies.

It is also important to take supplemental doses of acidophilus bacteria. Acidophilus is a "good" bacteria that helps build up the normal flora in the bowel as the yeast are being killed off. Other helpful steps would be to add anti-fungal foods such as garlic or garlic supplement and pau d'arco tea (also called lapacho, or tahebo tea).

There are many nutritional combinations that are offered in health food stores for the treatment of *candida*. However, if you wish to go beyond the above simple advice, it is best to consult with a naturopathic physician or a nutritionist.

HOT FLASHES OR POWER SURGES

Is it hot flushes or hot flashes? Some women who refuse to play victim call them "power surges."

A menopausal hot flash is a vasomotor reaction to hormonal shifts. Apparently LH (leuteinizing hormone) from the pituitary, which is designated to stimulate estrogen levels, is elevated at times of hot flashes. When the ovaries don't respond, the LH levels rise and a hot flash occurs. This ties in hot flashes with hormonal disturbances in the hypothalamus, the heat-regulatory center of the brain. There is also an increase in adrenal hormones at the time of the hot flash. To make matters worse, the sweat glands work less efficiently due to the decline in estrogen; therefore there is less cooling. So, as the thermostat in the brain decides the body is overheated, there is an increase of blood flow to the skin and it flushes red and creates perspiration. The evaporation of the sweat produced eventually causes cooling.

Women usually know when a hot flash is coming; there is an advance warning signal which is different for everyone, from a tingling sensation to nausea to a feeling of impending doom. A concentration of heat and tingling in the face, chest and upper body follows with perspiration which turns clammy and cold when the heat dissipates, usually within a few minutes.

Some sources say that there is a time frame with hot flashes, but everyone is different. Hot flashes can occur just as easily under stress as when resting. They occur during sleep and can contribute to fatigue and insomnia. The treatment here is not sleeping pills and antidepressants but attention to the hot flashes. Medically, estrogen is said to be the best treatment for this condition. However, there are many natural alternatives that also work and have no side effects.

Begin by keeping a journal to determine your own pattern of hot flashes. Then you can try to avoid the particular situations, foods or clothing that brought them on. Wear layers of clothing in natural fibers. Synthetics do not allow the skin to breathe. If all else fails, keep a fan or ice nearby.

The proper diet can help alleviate menopausal symptoms. Soy bean products are rich in phytosterols which provide hormonal building blocks for human hormones. Other foods that are high in phytoestrogens and progesterones include fruits such as apples, cherries, plums and coconuts; tubers such as carrots and yams; nightshades such as eggplant, tomatoes, potatoes and peppers (which may, however, exacerbate small joint arthritis); grains such as wheat germ, buckwheat and rice.

Supplements for Hot Flashes

The most important vitamin for menopause is:

- **Folic acid.** Dr. Robert Atkins has said that this nutrient "seems to produce an estrogen-like effect without side effects." The dosage that produces the desired effect, however, is only available on prescription. It can be from 5 mg to 20 mg daily.

Other helpful supplements include:

- **Desiccated adrenal,** one to two tablets twice a day, mid-morning and mid-afternoon.
- **Pantothenic acid,** a B vitamin that supports the adrenal glands, 500 mg three times a day.
- **B complex** for liver support, stress and nerve control. 50 mg one to two times per day.
- **Vitamin C,** which supports the adrenal glands, thereby reducing stress and hot flashes. It also supports the immune system. Take 1,000 mg two times a day.
- **Bioflavonoids** for relief of hot flashes, to prevent excessive menstrual flow and varicose veins. Also protects the heart. Take 500 mg daily.
- **Vitamin E,** 400 I.U. Take one to two per day, to protect the heart and aid the circulation and the functioning of the liver. Vitamin E oil can also be used locally to lubricate drying vaginal tissue.
- **Evening Primrose Oil** or **Black Currant Seed Oil,** taken as directed on the label. This acts as a sedative and a diuretic. It is recommended for hot flashes and is important for the production of estrogen.

Herbal Remedies
The best Chinese herbal patent medicine for menopause is called Women's Precious Pills or Eight Taste. It has antifungal properties as well as herbs to prevent hot flashes, vaginal dryness and anemia.

Flavonoid-rich herbs help restore vaginal lubrication, improve pelvic tone, strengthen the bladder, reduce water buildup in tissues, ease sore joints, decrease or end hot flashes, improve liver activity, lower risk of stroke and heart attack, reduce muscle cramping and improve resistance to infection. These herbs include horsetail, buckwheat greens, elderberries and flowers, hawthorn flowers and leaves, rose hips and flowers.

Herbs which promote progesterone production are best used when the menopausal menses come too frequently. These include chaste tree or vitex berries, sarsaparilla roots, wild yam roots, yarrow flowers and leaves. Consult *The Menopausal Years* by Susun Weed for more information about using herbs for menopause.

Siberian ginseng and dong quai are two of the most powerful menopausal herbs. Dong quai is an herb from the *angelica* species and its major medicinal use is for the treatment of "female" disorders. It is used for painful, scanty or excessive menstrual flow, menopausal symptoms and for pregnancy and delivery. Beyond these it is used for anemia, arthritis, migraines, abdominal pain and many other conditions. Dosage is usually one to three capsules per day.

Plant estrogens have been used for many centuries to treat conditions that are now treated by synthetic estrogens. Dong quai contains highly active phytoestrogens, but they function at a much lower level of activity than animal estrogens. They are only 1:400 times as active; that is, for the same measurable amount of synthetic estrogens you would have to have 400 times the amount of plant estrogens. Thus they are safe to take and bring with them no unpleasant side effects.

In fact, dong quai may be used for states of low estrogen as well as high estrogen. Phytoestrogens compete with estrogen for binding sites. When estrogen levels are low they act as replacement therapy. When estrogen levels are high the binding of plant estrogens to estrogen receptor sites blocks some of the excess effect of endogenous estrogen.

Angelica or dong quai is extremely safe with little or no side effects. However it does contain photoactive substances which may induce photosensitivity, so avoid excessive exposure to sunlight while using.

Ginseng acts as an adaptogen, which means it can balance abnormal physiology in an organism toward a normal healthy state. It has antifatigue properties and has a reputation among athletes for improving energy and endurance. It has antistress properties and has an effect on the hypothalamus or pituitary, promoting secretion of hormones that stimulate the adrenal glands. Ginseng has been shown to have anticancer and antiaging properties. It also stimulates the immune system and supports the liver's role in detoxification.

Ginseng is an excellent tonic for the menopausal woman since it supports the adrenals, the reproductive organs, the liver, the immune system, the nervous system—in fact most of the organs in the body.

Ginseng exerts estrogen-like action on the vaginal tissues. In fact it can prevent the thinning of the vagina which causes excessive drying, failure to lubricate and therefore painful intercourse.

The dosage depends on the percentage strength of the ginsenosides. The average dose is 4.6 grams per day in one to three doses. Since there are so many products on the market and no quality control, when you shop for ginseng look for at least 25 mg of ginsenoside per dose. Various practitioners suggest that if you wish to use ginseng for a prolonged period that you only use it for a two to three week period followed by a two to three week rest.

The following herbs, either alone or in combination are also helpful in treating menopause:

- **Black cohosh** has a long history of use in North America. It relieves hot flashes and is used for vaginal dryness. The root has estrogenic properties and has a normalizing effect on the female sex hormones. It is also a relaxant and is used for rheumatic pains.

- **Elder** contains bioflavins that aid the circulation and substances that can be used to treat rheumatism.

- **False unicorn** contains precursers to estrogen and normalizes hormone balance.

- **Licorice root** (not the candy) stimulates adrenal gland production. It contains substances similar to the natural steroids of the body. In menopause the adrenal glands are often overworked and need support.

- **Nettles** stimulate adrenal function, which strengthens and supports the whole body.

- **Wild yam** is the source for natural progesterone. It also comes in a topical cream.
- **Raspberry leaf** strengthens and tones the muscles of the uterus.
- **Sage** stimulates the muscles of the uterus.
- **Sarsaparilla** contains substances that stimulate testosterone activity in the body.

Most herbs are prepared by taking one to three teaspoons of dried herb to a pint of water, boiling gently for 30 minutes and drinking one to two cups a day. Consult the herbalist where you buy your supplies for specific directions since some products may require different preparations.

In general herbal teas are said to be more potent than capsules since the boiling releases more of the water-soluble properties. Even the extra fluid intake can be helpful to any health condition. However there are many herbal companies now that encapsulate herbs and claim similar results to herb teas. One advantage to capsules could be uniformity of product in terms of freshness, cleanliness, source, etc.

A teaspoon of **seaweed** daily may also help heal menopausal distress

Homeopathic Remedies
- **Belladonna** is used for flushed conditions with dilated pupils and bright red skin. It can also help the pounding headache that sometimes accompanies hot flushes.
- **Ignatia** suits women who are plagued with perfectionism. Menopause causes a lot of anger and irritability because it is so unpredictable and interferes with routine.
- **Lachesis** suits women who are very talkative and abhor tight clothing. They have sweating and flushing leading to severe headaches that feel like a constricting band pulling on the scalp.
- **Kreosotum** is important for burning symptoms. It can be used for burning vaginitis as well as for full body flushes and sweats that burn.
- **Pulsatilla** suits plump blond women who are teary and

sad. The hot flushes are mild to moderate and variable. The face may be flushed but the rest of the body cool.

• **Sepia** suits thin dark women who are bitter and depressed. The hot flushes may be severe and there is pressure in the lower extremities.

HORMONE REPLACEMENT THERAPY: YES OR NO?

For baby boomers in their mid-40s, estrogen therapy is a very hot topic. In keeping with our traditional drug-oriented way of handling female milestones, we are offered synthetic substitutes for the real thing. The optimal approach is to be drug-free, and with a healthy frame of mind and body, to greet this life change with open arms and heart. For the symptomatic woman, there are numerous natural alternatives, many of which are offered here.

The estrogen in HRT (Hormone Replacement Therapy) is synthetically manufactured, and your body must deal with it first as a synthetic and secondly as a hormone. The liver's job is to detoxify and eliminate anything that is not natural to the body; thus taking daily synthetic drugs puts unnecessary strain on the liver. This fact alone can contribute to aging and cause symptoms that are confused with menopause. To think that a synthetic hormone can mimic your own hormone action is a mistake. The same goes for synthetic progestins. They have numerous side effects, whereas natural progesterone has none.

If, after thorough research, estrogen and progesterone replacement are deemed necessary by you and your doctor, there are natural sources for both these hormones. Medical doctors practicing complementary medicine routinely prescribe these products. Unfortunately, since it is not possible to patent natural products, the drug companies do not want to spend the necessary money doing the clinical trials that would give us more proof of efficacy and safety.

HRT is itself an unproven therapy. Each new study that is done to try to reassure us that HRT is beneficial and harmless uncovers new reasons to be cautious. A recent study in *The New England Journal of Medicine* (June 15, 1995) studied 122,000 nurses and found a higher risk of breast cancer in those women taking the combined synthetic estrogen and progestin therapy. Progestins were added to estrogen to prevent women from getting uterine cancer, which is caused by taking estrogen alone.

According to Dr. Robert Atkins and others, there is a long list of contraindications to hormone replacement therapy. These include cardiovascular disease, diabetes, hypertension, high triglycerides, high cholesterol, tendency to weight gain, *Candidiasis*, stroke, smoking, fluid retention, liver disease, breast cancer, fibrocystic breast disease, thrombophlebitis, thromboembolism, unexplained vaginal bleeding, unexplained menstrual disorders, uterine fibroids, endometriosis, gallbladder disease and, of course, cancer. Dr. Atkins also recommends against estrogen if a woman suffers from any of the symptoms of hypoglycemia: fatigue, mood swings, depression, anxiety, irritability, panic attacks, cravings, seizure disorder, headaches, schizophrenia, confusion or other mental disorder, palpitations (mitral valve prolapse), bloating, multiple sclerosis, peptic ulcer or irritable bowel syndrome.

Besides uterine and breast cancer, synthetic estrogens are known to cause fluid retention and may increase the severity of asthma, heart disorders, kidney stones, epilepsy or migraine headaches. Estrogen can also stimulate the symptoms of hypoglycemia. In fact, Dr. Atkins has found that estrogen can convert low blood sugar into even lower blood sugar levels. It can convert asymptomatic hypoglycemia into a symptomatic form and it can cause even higher blood sugar levels in diabetics.

For those women who have tried everything else and still have symptoms, including women who have had surgical menopause, there are plant estrogens and progesterones that can be individually compounded by enlightened pharmacists. This type of estrogen therapy may be most useful for the low-estrogenic, thin, underdeveloped woman. The overweight woman may require only natural progesterone therapy.

There are, in fact, three active estrogens. These are estrone, estradiol and estriol. Estradiol (E2) is the main estrogen or true ovarian estrogen that is measured in the blood and the one usually used in North America for replacement therapy.

Estrone (E1) is the estrogen which is converted from androstenedione or estradiol by biosynthesis. Androstenedione is formed in the ovary, but its more important source is from the adrenal cortex. It is the adrenal gland that takes over some of the production of estrogen after menopause.

Estriol (E3) is an estrogen that is converted in the liver from estrone and also less directly from estradiol. A small amount of estriol may also be secreted by the ovary. Estriol is the main estrogen in pregnancy and enormous amounts are secreted by the placenta. The amount of estriol in the urine is evaluated as a test for pregnancy, the age of the fetus in the first trimester and the health of the fetus. Estriol is the safest form of estrogen.

Estrone has some reputation, although not proven, of being more carcinogenic than estradiol. Estrone was the main component of conjugated synthetic estrogens implicated in the rise of endometrial carcinoma in the 1970's. After 15 or 20 years of using conjugated estrogens it was determined that they were causing endometrial cancer.

When I was in medical school there was almost a moratorium on their use. "First do no harm" was the warning. Why would we give a strong hormone with such potent side effects to women for a condition that was not a disease? I wondered how we were to keep track of the future medical history of a woman who was given estrogen. In a gynecology lecture we were told not to give estrogen to someone with cancer. Then in pathology we learned that a cancer forms over a period from 5 to 15 years. How could we predict who would develop breast cancer or endometrial cancer in the year or two after they filled our prescription with a medication that was potentially carcinogenic?

Another question deeply concerned me. I wondered if there was any cumulative effect from taking the birth control pill for 5, 10 or 15 years and subsequently taking conjugated estrogens. There is no research that I know of that is even considering this question. How does the body respond to long-term use of a synthetic hormone that tries to mimic a natural hormone? How does a synthetic affect all the biochemical mechanisms in the body? There are so many unanswered questions, and unfortunately we are allowing medical technology and the pharmaceutical industry to proceed without giving us any answers. I do not want to find in another 15 or 20 years that we have made yet another mistake.

In 1978, Dr. A. H. Follingstad wrote in the *Journal of the American Medical Association*:

> All present commercial and popular orally administered estrogens are estrone, combinations of estrone and estradiol, or estradiol alone. Moreover, it has been shown that orally administered estradiol, including the micronized form, is mainly converted to estrone in the small bowel, thus making all the usual orally administered estrogens, in effect, estrone.
>
> . . . In our country [estriol] has been labeled a weak or ineffective estrogen and difficult if not impossible to obtain. Actually it is not weak if given in adequate doses. A dose of two to four mg is equivalent of 0.6 to 1.25 mg of conjugated estrogen or estrone and is just as effective. It has been available in Europe for many years and is cited in articles on the equivalent doses of various estrogens. Estriol does not lose its unique identity when given orally as does estradiol; it remains estriol.

The more I hear about estriol the more convinced I am that women can take HRT and make it a very safe experience. Estriol does not cause build-up of the endometrial lining and periodic menstrual shedding as does synthetic estrogen yet it eliminates hot flashes and vaginal atrophy.

Another hormone that is finally being researched, mostly as an antiaging drug, is DHEA. It is labeled an androgen, which we equate more with male hormones like testosterone, but women produce androgens as well as men. Androgens improve bone density and bone strength. According to Dr. Guy Abraham, 50 mg of DHEA given to postmenopausal women improved the sense of well being in 85 percent of the women and improved immunocompetence and bone metabolism. DHEA, Dr. Abraham says, has no negative effects on lipids and insulin. There is much interest in this hormone, and more research will elucidate its true role in the treatment of menopause.

Dr. Serifina Corsello is a remarkable physician practising in New York City who understands the relationship of underlying stress and infections as they impact upon the menopausal years. Her therapies for menopause include new, innovative techniques to cleanse and heal the body; she also has perfected the art of natural HRT.

Dr. Corsello first obtains hormonal blood levels. Since the progesterone is usually very low, she begins by using natural progesterone cream. The dosage could be as high as one teaspoon twice per day for three months. Any menopausal symptoms usually subside and the blood levels are retested. If the progesterone is not high enough, oral natural progesterone is prescribed and the cream dosage is lowered. Adjustments are made over the ensuing months until the correct balance is achieved.

If progesterone does not alleviate all symptoms or the woman has been on Premarin and wishes to be on natural estrogen, a slow process of lowering the Premarin while raising natural estrogen begins. Then the very low dose of Premarin is replaced with either estriol or a tri-estrogen which includes estradiol-estrone, but mostly estriol.

It may seem like a slow process compared with the usual pharmaceutical approach but that is the way of natural medicine which allows the body to adapt and rebalance gradually.

PREVENTING OSTEOPOROSIS

Women at risk for osteoporosis are small, inactive, thin Northern European, light haired, light skinned, have a sedentary lifestyle, smoke, drink too much alcohol and coffee, have a long history of poor diet and low intake of calcium and vitamin D, a history of cortisone treatment, a family history of osteoporosis, were never pregnant, have periodontal disease, and a history of aluminum antacid intake. Premenopausal removal of ovaries with loss of estrogen and testosterone is of course a big factor also. Once again, many of the above risk factors are under our personal control. Knowing them makes us much more aware of our own responsibility for our own good health.

The herbalist Susun Weed has reported in her book *The Menopausal Years* some very interest facts about osteoporosis:

> For about five years, right after menopause, the bones apparently reject calcium and osteoporosis increases, giving rise to the belief that ERT, taken as soon as menopause begins and continued for several decades, is the only hope for women who want to avoid broken bones ... But bones start absorbing calcium once again when this "Bone-pause" is past.

Susun then explains why this is so:

> When you take ERT, bone cell creation is not improved. Bone cell death is slowed down, suppressed. Unfortunately the rate of bone loss can increase greatly if you stop taking ERT. When you build bones with green allies [vegetables] and exercise, bone cell creation is stimulated and supported. If you must eat poorly or miss your physical activity for some weeks, bone mass is still retained.

Susun really puts things into perspective when she reminds us that "Bone loss during one premenopausal month without menses is the equivalent of one year's bone loss postmenopausally."

Women on HRT need to be wary of abnormal vaginal bleeding, new lumps and bumps and any aches and pains. They may need to have more mammograms and that has its risks too. Endometrial biopsies are advised for women on HRT to make sure there is no buildup of abnormal cells in the endometrial lining of the uterus. All these procedures, office visits and medications to deal with side effects are very costly and can also be emotionally draining.

A wonderful piece of insight comes from Agnes Whistling Elk in *Women at the Edge of Two Worlds* by Lynn Andrews. She says, "When you lose your intent, your will to structure your life, you lose bone." Menopause can be a time of growth and accomplishment, but it is we who have to set our goals.

TREATMENTS FOR PREVENTING OSTEOPOROSIS

Exercise

Daily vigorous walks are an excellent exercise. To protect your knees and hips try jogging on a mini-trampoline.

Yoga and tai chi are excellent ways to create flexibility and strength as they promote an inner calm and balance.

Biking, swimming, playing tennis, gardening, etc., will stimulate your whole body to work and feel better. You will sleep better and metabolize better.

It is never too late to build dense flexible bones, and it is never too soon. In fact, your best insurance for a fracture-free, strong-boned post-menopause is to build bone mass before menopause. The more exercise and bone minerals you get in your younger years, the more ultimate benefit you will reap. The more bone mass you have by age 40, the more you'll have at 55 and the more you'll have at 75 when it really counts.

Supplements

Calcium supplementation should be considered along with calcium-rich foods as estrogen levels decline. Calcium plays a vital role in many basic physiological processes, including blood coagulation, the sending of messages along nerves, maintenance of muscle tone, preservation of cell membrane integrity and permeability and certain glandular functions. Soft-tissue calcium is replenished either by absorption of dietary calcium or by robbing calcium from the bone stores. Over the long term, robbing calcium from the bones can lead to thin, weakened bone and possible bone fracture. Thus it is important to keep your dietary calcium high.

• **Calcium** and **magnesium** are very important even before menopause to prevent osteoporosis. They can be introduced and used at any time after age 30, but should be continued indefinitely: calcium, 1,000 to 1,500 mg, magnesium 500 mg per day if no dairy products are eaten. Magnesium has a laxative action when taken on its own, but combined with calcium in the same tablet, this effect is attenuated.

• **Microcystalline Hydroxyapatite (MCHC)** is a new calcium supplement which offers prevention and repair of bone loss. MCHC is a bone food that provides calcium in an extremely bioavailable form. MCHC is a whole bone extract (food), but not a bone meal. It is processed at a very low temperature, thereby retaining the delicate calcium-protein matrix which is so important to its effectiveness. In tests, MCHC as a bone food has been shown actually to produce a significant increase in bone mass, which has not been demonstrated with any other form of calcium. MCHC is extremely well-absorbed and is ideal for young and old alike.

• **Boron** is a mineral which is usually added to MCHC formulas because it has been implicated as a valuable nutrient for the promotion of proper calcium metabolism and prevention of urinary calcium loss.

Christiane Northrup M.D., in her book, *Women's Bodies Women's Wisdom*, recommends 2 to 12 mg per day of boron. She notes that besides reducing urinary calcium loss, boron increases levels of estradiol in the blood which helps promote bone health. Organic fruits, vegetables and nuts are the best sources of boron.

Other Nutrients
• **Sunshine** 20 minutes a day for the beneficial effects of *Vitamin D*, a prohormone necessary for the absorption of calcium.

• **Vitamin K,** also crucial to calcium absorption. Good sources are potatoes, yogurt, molasses, leafy greens, green tea, kelp, and nettles.

Calcium and Magnesium-Rich Herbs
- **Alfalfa, nettle, oatstraw, kelp, horsetail** and **sage.**

Calcium Rich Foods

Emphasize high-calcium protein sources such as tahini, tofu, oats, seaweed, sardines and salmon (with the bones) yogurt, oatmeal, dandelion leaves, dark leafy greens such as collards, kale and broccoli. The highest incidence of osteoporosis is found in the Scandinavian countries, where the consumption of dairy products and meat are the highest.

As a person ages, it is important to cut back on protein intake and dairy products and to increase enzymes in the body by eating foods high in enzymes such as papaya or pineapple or to take *enzyme tablets* and *hydrochloric acid* to aid digestion and food breakdown.

It may seem contradictory to reduce dairy products just when the need for calcium is greatest. However, many people are allergic to dairy products which in their homogenized and pasteurized form are difficult to digest. You must see for yourself what your body prefers.

Other Helpful Hints

Calcium requires an acid environment for maximum digestibility. To increase hydrochloric acid production for digestion of calcium, iron and other nutrients, try any of the following:

- Drink lemon juice in water with or after your meal.
- Take 10–15 drops of *dandelion root tincture* in several ounces of water about fifteen minutes before you eat.
- Add two tablespoons apple cider vinegar and two tablespoons raw honey or blackstrap molasses to a cup of hot water; drink with or after your meal.

Bone Antagonists

Foods which impede calcium absorption include caffeine, soda pop (because of phosphorus), white sugar, white flour products, excess protein and processed meats. Tobacco, alcohol and fiber pills also inhibit calcium absorption. Other factors affecting calcium absorption include tetracycline and other antibiotics, low hydrochloric acid (HCL) levels, low thyroid production and the use of aluminum cookware and products containing aluminum such as baking powder and underarm deodorants.

The digestion of protein produces acids which are buffered with calcium when excreted in the urine. Thus foods rich in protein but low in calcium (such as red meat) result in calcium loss from the bones.

Excess salt in the diet produces urine loaded with calcium. Women eating 3,900 mg of sodium daily excreted 30 percent more calcium than those eating 1,600 mg daily (*British Medical Journal* 299, 1989). Table salt is rarely the problem; the main sources of dietary sodium are processed and canned foods. Seaweed is an excellent, calcium-rich source of salt.

Natural Progesterone

A very exciting breakthrough in osteoporosis treatment is the use of a cream containing natural progesterone extracted from wild yams. One teaspoon applied to the skin twice per day is said to prevent bone loss. The skin cream is efficiently absorbed through the skin, which avoids the first-pass liver loss of oral medications. This accounts for its freedom from side effects.

Dr. John Lee studied the effects of natural progesterone cream on 100 patients with osteoporosis. The patients were postmenopausal white females ranging in age from 38 to 83. The average age at the entry point was 65.2 years of age. The average time from menopause was 16 years. All women were followed for more than three years and 63 percent had their bone status evaluated with serial dual photon absorptiometry during this time.

The results of treatment were found to be consistently beneficial. By the third month of treatment, patients were reporting an improved sense of well-being. Over the three-year observation period patients' height stabilized, aches and pains diminished, mobility and energy levels rose, normal sexual desire returned. There were no negative side effects nor any rise in the lipid levels as compared to reports with some synthetic progestin trials.

Bone density studies were performed at six months or one year intervals and showed a progressive increase. The faster increases occurred in those with the lowest initial bone densities. The occurrence of osteoporotic fractures dropped to zero. Three traumatic bone fractures healed well, and the treating orthopedists commented on the excellent bone structure of these patients.

Dr. Lee concluded:

> Present osteoporosis management emphasizes prevention rather than cure since true reversal has proven unobtainable by conventional methods. With the hypothesis that progesterone is the missing ingredient for normal bone-building in women, transdermal progesterone cream supplementation (with or without estrogen) was tested in an office-based setting over the past six years. Treatment resulted in progressive increase in bone mineral density and, more importantly, definite clinical improvement as evidenced by pain relief, height stabilization, increased physical activity, and fracture prevention. The benefits achieved were found to be independent of age. It is concluded that osteoporosis reversal is a clinical reality in a program that is safe, uncomplicated, and inexpensive.
>
> Postmenopausal supplementation with progesterone or estrogen balanced with natural progesterone cream imposes no increased risks regarding cardiovascular disease, breast cancer or endometrial cancer. In fact, natural progesterone is almost certainly protective.

More studies need to be undertaken to compare natural hormone replacement with synthetic hormone replacement.

In summary, my personal regimen for the treatment of menopausal symptoms would begin with the Chinese herbal preparation called Women's Precious Pills; if symptoms continue I would add estriol and natural progesterone pills. For preventing osteoporosis, I suggest daily exercise, a calcium/ magnesium supplement and natural progesterone cream.

PREVENTING HEART DISEASE

Research has shown that fully 90 percent of existing heart disease could be avoided with lifestyle improvements and alternative therapies. Regular aerobic exercise, a nutrient- and fiber-rich low fat diet and healthy ways to relieve stress top the list as far as preventive measures are concerned. One of the best books on this subject is *Preventing and Reversing Heart Disease* by Dean Ornish, M.D.

Even though there is speculation that estrogen is protective against heart disease since women before menopause have a lower incidence of heart disease than after menopause, estrogen replacement therapy may expose women to more risks than benefits. There are still too few studies and far too many unanswered questions to justify using synthetic estrogens after menopause as a defense against heart disease.

The Importance of Diet

Extra weight puts a strain on the heart because the heart has to pump blood to all the extra capillaries that feed the extra tissue. For those who are overweight or who have elevated blood lipids, a diet such as the Ornish diet or the Pritikin diet, which derives just 10 percent of its calories from fat, is recommended. For those who are still healthy and want to stay that way, a diet with 20 to 25 percent of fat calories would be appropriate. Most important for everyone is a menu rich in fresh vegetables, fish, whole grains (such as oatmeal, brown rice and whole grain breads), legumes and fruits. Avoid sugar and processed and refined foods.

Exercise

Exercise is the most effective route to permanent weight loss and a healthy heart and circulatory system; moreover, it is a natural stress reducer. You needn't buy expensive equipment or join a gym. A brisk half hour walk each day, gradually increasing your gait, will bring enormous health benefits not only to your heart, but to your lungs, your bones and your sense of well-being.

Bad Habits

Smoking of course is out. It dramatically decreases the oxygen level throughout the body and the heart has to work furiously in order to keep the body oxygenated. More than an occasional alcoholic drink is also toxic to the heart, and caffeine is implicated in a number of cardiac problems such as rapid or irregular heartbeat and elevated blood pressure.

Helpful Supplements and Herbs

The following supplements may be used preventively or therapeutically. Consult a nutritionally oriented physician for the program that is right for you.

- **Vitamin C,** two grams per day as an antioxidant
- **Vitamin E,** 400–800 units per day as an antioxidant
- **Magnesium,** 500 mg per day for heart spasms and palpitations
- **B Complex,** 50 mg to calm the nervous system, one or two per day
- **A good multiple vitamin and mineral**

The herbs that are useful for the heart are

- **Hawthorn berry or crataegus** as an herbal tincture. Use 5 to 10 drops in four ounces of water three times a day.
- **Spigelia** as an herbal tincture for severe chest pain. This should not be used in place of prescribed medication. Both the tinctures and medication can be used but one should not take chances with a life-threatening situation by trying stubbornly to use only natural remedies.
- **Avena sativa** tincture to help treat palpitations. Use 5 to 10 drops three or four times a day. The most common

cause of heart palpitations is coffee intake, and that should be stopped.

An alternative but invasive method for treating atherosclerosis, angina and heart disease is chelation therapy. An intravenous injection of a mineral-binding agent removes the mineral/cholesterol plaque from the artery walls. In numerous studies this has proven beneficial in reversing heart disease.

NATURAL REMEDIES FOR OTHER MENOPAUSAL COMPLAINTS

Following is a compilation of menopausal symptoms and symptoms related to aging, with solutions and remedies to enable you to take responsibility for your own health. All too often, after the age of 45, women are told, "Well, what do you expect; you're getting old," or "It must be the menopause." Unfortunately this approach ignores or misdiagnoses treatable symptoms.

ADDICTIONS

As part of the menopausal detoxification process, addictions must be addressed. Coffee, alcohol and tobacco all contribute to worsening of menopausal symptoms.

The treatment of addictions encompasses diet, remedies and behavioral and psychological counseling. Following are some of the remedies that can be useful in this process.

Coffee

First, switch to black tea and take *chamomilla* 30c; a homeopathic remedy for withdrawal symptoms of irritability, sensitivity and headaches. The dosage is four drops orally three or four times a day and should not exceed six days in duration. Then black tea is stopped and *chamomilla* can be continued for another few days. Finally, switch from black tea to herbal teas or one of the grain coffee substitutes that are available in health food stores.

Smoking

For this addiction the remedies are:

• **Caladium, nicotine** and **tabac,** all homeopathics in the 6x or 6c potency, four drops taken three to six times a day.

• The herbal tinctures **lobelia** or **avena sativa** taken 5–10 drops in four ounces of water three times a day.

• A remedy called **calc phos** used in the 6c potency for residual bronchitis that may remain after giving up cigarettes.

• **Fenugreek seed** tea, one teaspoon per cup of boiling water steeped for seven minutes. This can help loosen the mucus that accompanies cigarette withdrawal.

The first month or so after quitting is often a difficult time. The small hair cells that line the bronchial tracts are beginning to grow again after being paralyzed for so long and they start creating and clearing a lot of mucus. This is a good sign.

Ear acupuncture can be done in order to help curb the craving for nicotine and to calm the irritability that usually ensues.

The other basic advice would be to maintain a good diet, avoiding red meat, sugar, coffee and refined foods, and taking a good multiple vitamin and mineral as well as **zinc.** Zinc at 30–50 mg a day will help bring back the taste buds so that food may be enjoyed more fully. Try to avoid switching one addiction for another. Most people who give up smoking begin eating sweets and gaining weight. Try to understand the reason for the addiction and avoid being dependent on any substance.

Alcohol

Addiction to alcohol can be treated with homeopathic **sulfuric acid** 6c, four drops every few hours. This remedy is completely safe and has none of the properties of full potency sulfuric acid in this extremely dilute form. It acts like Antabuse, a medical drug which is used to create a feeling of nausea and illness if a person drinks while taking this substance.

A rare remedy called **quarkus alba** can curb the desire for alcohol, and **nux vomica** can curb desire as well as treat a hangover. Take four drops every hour for a hangover and three to four times a day to prevent desire for alcohol.

High doses of **vitamin C** will help metabolize alcohol after ingestion but should not be used so a person can drink more. High doses would mean 2 to 8 grams throughout the day.

Alcoholism, a psychological and physical addiction, has to be treated in a whole person manner. An excellent diet of grains, vegetables, fish, chicken and fruit which avoids refined foods, sugar, coffee and tea will stop the craving for alcohol. Some people feel that low blood sugar can trigger addiction to sugar or alcohol.

Vitamin therapy would consist of the already mentioned high doses of **vitamin C;** high doses of **niacinamide (B3),** 500 mg, from two to eight a day; **vitamin B6**, 100 mg, three times a day; and a **B complex,** 50 mg, two or three times a day. **Zinc** is also important, 50 mg per day for a month and then reduce to 25 mg per day plus a good **multiple vitamin and mineral supplement.**

Read the section on **Hypoglycemia,** which is biochemically related to alcoholism, since alcohol is a form of sugar.

ARTHRITIS

Arthritis is inflammation of the joints. This is a very complex syndrome which is very relevant to the menopausal woman.

At menopause, women often begin to get arthritic symptoms. As mentioned earlier in the section on detoxification, I suspect that the absence of the monthly period, which served to rid the body of toxins, is to blame. Perhaps at menopause the toxins build and lodge in the joints. For this reason, I advise patients to go through detoxification (see page 6).

Treatment for arthritis includes a good healthy diet of

whole grains, vegetables, nuts, seeds, fruit, fish and chicken. To begin, one should eliminate the most allergenic foods such as wheat, dairy, corn and sugar and determine if there is an improvement. If not, eliminate the most likely yeast-growing foods such as sugar, bread with yeast, moldy foods, cheeses and excess fruits and see if it changes the joint symptoms. A common cause of small-joint arthritis is allergy to the deadly nightshade family of potato, tomato, green pepper, tobacco, eggplant and paprika. These should be avoided for at least two months to determine possible allergy.

Simple advice for relief includes:

• Castor oil compresses or rubs. Castor oil has been proven to increase lymphatic blood flow and to clear away toxins and inflammatory by-products.

• Gentle stretches and exercise such as tai chi and yoga are especially helpful. Hydrotherapy in a heated pool can do wonders as can swimming or gentle exercise in a pool. Massage therapy helps the circulation and helps clear away inflammatory by-products.

• Simple meditation, prayer or affirmations help to calm and remove stress. The Silva Method is a non-religious meditation-affirmation technique that has an excellent world-wide reputation.

• Be careful with heating pads and ice. Use heat only on stiff joints and for only a short time. Use ice if a joint is hot and inflamed. Be sure to check with your doctor for special instructions in your particular case.

Supplements that help arthritic symptoms are:

• **Vitamin C,** one gram three times a day.

• **Pancreatic enzymes,** two tablets three times a day. This, in conjunction with vitamin C, acts as an anti-inflammatory which has proven to be as effective as most anti-inflammatory medications.

• **B vitamins,** such as

• **Niacinamide,** 500 mg two to six tablets a day

• **Vitamin B6,** 100 mg one to three times a day.

Some people also respond to the herb

• **Devil's claw,** two to six capsules per day.

- **Evening primrose oil** and **fish oils** have demonstrated improved joint mobility and decreased inflammation. They are natural anti-inflammatories.

There are also many homeopathic remedies for arthritis. Since it is a chronic condition, however, it requires the skills of a homeopathic physician to take the case history and prescribe the best remedy.

BACK PAIN

This can be a frightening condition that signals anything from a muscle spasm to a crushed vertebra due to osteoporosis or a prolapsed or slipped disc. This occurs when the pad between each vertebra is forced out from between the vertebrae and the bones are crushing or pressing the nerves that branch off the spinal cord. The diagnosis definitely has to be clarified. If the advice is limited bed rest, muscle relaxants and pain killers, a person can also use ice alternating with heat. The following homeopathic remedies can be useful and are nontoxic:

- **Arnica** 6c for pain, shock and swelling, four drops every half to one hour while pain is severe.
- **Rhus tox** 6c can be used if the pain is more like stiffness.
- **Hypericum** 6c can be used in the same amounts, if there is a definite nerve tingling and irritation.

The best treatment for pain in the acute injury period is ice. Never use heat on an acute inflammation. If the pain is chronic, use ice first, then heat (ten minutes of one, rest ten minutes and ten minutes of the other).

Castor oil packs for both acute and chronic pain are excellent. Take an old hand towel and rub in four to five tablespoons of castor oil. Cover the affected area but ensure that your bed clothes are protected with plastic. You may use a heating pad on low to help the action, but the pack works just fine at room temperature too. Leave on at least one hour or overnight. Castor oil has been proven to reduce inflammation. Warm to moderately hot epsom salts baths will also help chronic back pain.

The nutrients for easing back pain are high doses of

- **Vitamin C,** from 2 to 5 grams a day;
- **Calcium** and **magnesium** in a one-to-one ratio, 500 mg each, one to two a day.

Acupuncture is effective for the treatment of back pain and so are gentle and structured exercises. If a person is overweight, the excess weight can aggravate the problem, so a weight-loss program is indicated. Several recent studies have proven that the best care for acute and chronic back pain is treatment by a good chiropractor.

BLADDER INFECTIONS

Because the lower lining of the urethra is somewhat like the anatomy of the vagina, infections occur in that region as well. The infection in the urethra that carries the worst consequences is carried by *e. coli* bacteria which can ascend into the bladder, leading to cystitis, bladder infection or minor infection symptoms such as unusual urinary frequency.

For anyone suffering from chronic or frequent bladder infection, the book *You Don't Have to Live With Cystitis* by Dr. Larrian Gillespie is a wonderful source of information. There are chapters on how to deal with acute and chronic infection, information on the allergic causes of bladder symptoms and advice on all aspects of bladder and kidney disease.

During the years when you don't know if your periods have completely stopped you must still use birth control. If you are using a diaphragm, it can be the cause of problems, and can also lead to bladder infections.

If bladder symptoms begin, such as frequent urination, burning and pressure, it is important to submit a urine sample to your doctor so that it may be tested for bacterial overgrowth. While waiting for results, the natural treatment might include:

- One-half to one-fourth teaspoon baking soda in a glass of water every 30 minutes. This can help make the urine less acidic and therefore less burning.
- **Crantabs,** six to eight per day.
- Avoidance of tea and coffee.

- Drinking **parsley** or **chamomile** tea in large quantities to help treat the condition.
- **Uva ursi** capsules, two to three times a day.
- Drinking lots of water to flush out bacteria.
- Taking homeopathic remedies such as **cantharis** or **causticum** in the 6c or 30c potency every hour can be helpful.
- If you have a post-coital irritation, take **staphasagria** 6 or 30 c every hour.

Do not drink chamomile tea if you are taking homeopathic remedies because it can neutralize them.

Simple common sense advice to prevent bladder infections includes avoiding tight synthetic undergarments or pants; wearing loose cotton underwear; avoiding scented tampons, pads or even colored toilet paper. After a bowel movement wipe from front to back to avoid pulling bowel bacteria into the vagina-urethra area.

Studies show that pure cranberry juice or cranberry juice tablets help bladder infections. If you must take an antibiotic, ask your doctor for a urinary antiseptic such as nitrofurantoin or nalidixic acid which does not affect the intestinal bacteria or cause *candidiasis*. If you have to use an antibiotic be sure to take acidophilus tablets as well.

DEPRESSION

Depression may have multiple causes and require multiple treatments. As in all other conditions, optimal nutrition, proper vitamin supplementation, exercise and sleep are the basis for any natural approach. Frequently, people with a major stress or grief will find that they are unable to sleep and will stop exercising and stop eating properly. This perpetuates a cycle of improper care for the body which can prolong or deepen the condition. Try not to get too discouraged about feeling low because it will only make you feel worse. Try to exercise or go out and do something fun, especially with other people. Sharing your dreams with a friend or counsellor can often help you understand why you're depressed. Talking about it usually helps.

Studies have shown that most depression does not occur in the menopausal age group. However, if a woman becomes depressed in her 50's, it is often blamed on menopause. Depression is often a result of low blood sugar or hypoglycemia. See page 39.

DRY SKIN

Dry skin is not necessarily due to menopause, nor is it cured by estrogen replacement therapy, nor can it be corrected by external cream applications. The diet and what is taken orally are most important. Some suggestions to treat dry skin include:

- **Evening primrose oil** and **fish oils,** in amounts of three to four capsules a day. Alternatively take one tablespoon of **flaxseed oil** daily.
- **Cod liver oil,** which can be taken in liquid form, one teaspoon daily.
- **Zinc** supplementation of 25 mg a day for skin, hair and nails.
- **Multiple vitamin and mineral.**

In terms of skin care, some people feel that too many showers and baths strip the normal acid mantle of the skin and promote dehydration and drying of the skin. This can be treated by putting a few tablespoons of apple cider vinegar in the bath and by using neutral pH skin creams.

Drinking enough water is also very important—from six to eight glasses a day. This rehydrates the skin. One of the simplest things that any person can do for overall good health, including the skin, is to drink more pure water.

FATIGUE

One of the most frequent complaints brought to doctors by their patients is fatigue. Fatigue can be caused by a multitude of problems such as low-grade untreated infection, anemia, adrenal stress or immune system depression. In menopause, fatigue can also be due to the lack of sleep because of hot flushes.

If you are bothered by symptoms of menopause then it may be safe to say that your adrenal glands are overworked. This may be due to poor diet, smoking, overconsumption of alcohol, overwork or lack of proper rest. Lifestyle changes can make a huge difference in your stress levels. A good diet, regular exercise plus eight hours sleep at night will go a long way to improve your general health.

Treatment for overworked adrenals includes vitamin C, two to ten grams per day, pantothenic acid 500 mg per day, desiccated adrenal 80 mg, two to four per day and herbs such as gota kola, ginseng in capsule form (two to three per day). Red Korean ginseng is especially suited for women.

Exercise is extremely important for balancing stress. However, because of menopausal fatigue some women avoid exercise, which perpetuates a vicious cycle. It is important to remember that exercise can actually banish some forms of fatigue.

FIBROIDS

Fibroids are benign overgrowths of the muscles in the wall of the uterus caused by hormonal imbalance. During menopause fibroids actually shrink. So, if you have fibroids, you should look forward to menopause.

In the perimenopausal interval, fibroids can still stretch the uterus lining, which can cause heavier bleeding and more cramping during the period. The medical treatment is often a hysterectomy if symptoms of bleeding or pain are debilitating. There is a lot of controversy around the removal of fibroids.

The treatment up to the point of surgery is difficult to delineate because there has been very little research on the treatment of fibroids. Dr. John Lee has done the most impressive work to date. He says that fibroids are a product of the estrogen dominance that occurs when a woman does not ovulate at midcycle. Without ovulation, progesterone is not formed, and estrogen dominates and stimulates the growth of breast cysts and fibroids. Dr. Lee states that when sufficient progesterone is replaced, fibroids no longer grow; they decrease in size and finally, at menopause, they shrink altogether. Blood levels of progesterone can help you and your doctor determine how much progesterone you need.

Since estrogenic hormones seem to stimulate fibroid growth and fats are a precursor to estrogen, a low saturated fat diet, optimally vegetarian, is beneficial. Avoid meat, dairy, alcohol, coffee, chocolate, sugar, salt, fried or fatty foods and anything processed or refined.

Fats and nutrients essential to the body should come from unsaturated fatty acids such as:

- **Evening primrose oil,** four capsules per day
- **Marine lipid capsules,** four per day
- **Vitamin E,** 400 I.U. per day
- **Vitamin A,** 20,000 I.U. per day
- **Multiple vitamin and mineral**
- **Bioflavonoids** and **vitamin C.** These are very important to lessen the heavy bleeding accompanying fibroids. Two to four grams of each may be necessary.

Foot reflexology massage has helped diminish the pain caused by fibroids and in some cases even diminished fibroids. External castor oil packs or bentonite clay poultices can ease the pain and congestion created by the fibroids.

Herbal formulas that might help shrink fibroids or relieve heavy bleeding include a combination of herbs such as *vitex agnus castus* (chaste tree berry), dong quai, licorice root, *dioscorea* (wild yam) and sarsaparilla. It is best to consult an herbalist for an appropriate formula.

If fibroids become debilitating, find a doctor who is willing, if at all possible, to remove the fibroid alone without removing the uterus. This is often possible with very large fibroids which are in a good position to be removed. An excellent book on this topic is *No More Hysterectomies* by Dr. Vicki Hufnagel.

Headaches

The most common types of headaches are tension, migraine, hypoglycemic, allergic, chronic fatigue and headaches following head trauma or injury. In menopause, existing headache patterns can be exacerbated. On the other hand, hormonally triggered headaches may cease—unless, of course, one replenishes decreasing hormone levels with HRT.

One of the best treatments for headaches is deep muscle massage to try to break down the calcification, increase the circulation to the head and return normal function.

Chiropractic adjustment is often necessary to release the cervical vertebrae, but adequate attention must be paid to the muscle component. It is often muscles in spasm that are pulling the vertebrae out of alignment, and frequent adjustments are not going to help if the muscles remain in spasm.

Migraine headaches have a component of light sensitivity, nausea and sometimes vomiting. Elimination of cigarette smoke, pork, oranges, wheat, eggs, chocolate, dairy, sugar, beef, tea and coffee can account for 85 percent relief of symptoms. Keep a food diary since any food could be the culprit.

An herb called **feverfew** is sometimes helpful in alleviating headaches and may be tried as a preventative, two to six capsules per day before the headaches occur.

Calcium and **magnesium** may be used to relax muscles and for pain relief.

Heavy Menstrual Bleeding

This condition is quite common at the perimenopausal time. The following supplements may be helpful:
- **Bioflavonoids** (especially **rutin**) to strengthen veins and capillaries and slow down excessive flow, one to three grams daily, cutting back as the bleeding lessens.
- **Vitamin A,** 25,000 I.U. daily
- **Chelated iron,** 25 to 50 mg daily

- **GLA (evening primrose oil** or **borage oil),** two capsules, three times daily
- **Vitamin K,** 10 mg daily

Note that subclinical hypothyroidism can be an underlying reason for heavy bleeding. In this case, kelp, iodine drops or even desiccated thyroid may be necessary, but only on the recommendation of a holistic physician.

Herbal combinations including **licorice root, alfalfa, vitex agnus castus, dong quai, wild yam** and **sarsaparilla** might also be very helpful. It is best to consult an herbalist.

If none of these measures work, a holistic physician might prescribe a trial of estriol and natural progesterone tailored to your menstrual cycle.

HYPOGLYCEMIA

The understanding and treatment of hypoglycemia is pivotal in the proper management of many menopausal symptoms.

In premenopausal women, carbohydrate metabolism is affected by the decreased progesterone secretion in the second half of the menstrual cycle. This leads to changes in the tolerance to sugar, so that the blood sugar level does not have to drop very much in order to produce hunger. When this happens, women tend to eat more and crave more sugar and carbohydrates.

Stress, sugar and caffeine put a burden on the adrenal glands, causing them to overwork. The cessation of ovulation places a special burden on the endocrine system, and hypoglycemia is the result.

Some of the symptoms of hypoglycemia include headaches, dizziness, eye focusing problems, mood swings—especially depression—irritability, food cravings and insomnia.

The adrenal glands are affected by hypoglycemia in the following way: as sugar or caffeine is taken, the blood sugar rises sharply, causing the pancreas to work extra hard to put out more insulin to force the excess sugar into the cells. A seesaw effect can occur when the blood sugar drops too low. At this point the adrenal glands surge to push the blood sugar back up. This surge can be felt as an anxiety attack or panicky feeling.

The adrenals especially need to be supported at menopause because they take over the job of the ovaries in producing female hormones. If the adrenal glands are exhausted from trying to balance the blood sugar, it might be more difficult for this hormone production to occur. Other stressful situations, such as allergies, asthma, anxiety and the use of cortisone medications, can also cause adrenal gland exhaustion.

When we compare hypoglycemia symptoms and menopausal symptoms, from mood swings to sugar cravings to fatigue, the similarities are striking. Obviously not all women exhibit all symptoms; each patient has her own inherent weaknesses.

The treatment for hypoglycemia is small frequent meals of complex carbohydrates (vegetables, whole grains, legumes) and protein. There are doctors who suggest emphasizing either one or the other but I think it is important to balance them. Avoid sugars and refined foods and limit your fruit intake. It may be worthwhile to sit down with a nutritional counsellor to devise proper diet management of this condition.

Supplements that are helpful in treating hypoglycemia are:
- **A good multi-vitamin and mineral.**
- **B vitamins,** 50 mg one to two a day in a nonyeast base to support the nervous system.
- **Pantothenic acid,** a B vitamin which supports the adrenal glands, 500 mg one to three a day for those people whose adrenal glands are exhausted.
- **Desiccated adrenal** can also be used for a short time, one to two tablets at midmorning and midafternoon.
- **Chromium,** a mineral which has been shown to assist glucose tolerance and balance, 200 mg per day.

HYPOTHYROIDISM

The thyroid gland is located on either side of the trachea in the neck. Because it controls the metabolism of all the cells of the body, it affects the production of progesterone from cholesterol. If the thyroid is low or hypo, then the metabolic rate is lowered and there is less progesterone produced. Also, if the thyroid is low, this indicates that the adrenal glands are also in a weakened condition.

A person can become sluggish, fatigued, have difficulty waking up in the morning, be overweight, have coarsening of the hair and skin, be constipated and have more frequent infections, irregularity of periods and poor wound healing. Since these symptoms overlap with many other conditions, it is important to make an accurate diagnosis. Unfortunately, the blood tests for the thyroid tend to be inaccurate and also can miss an early case of low thyroid.

During menopause the thyroid can be placed under unusual strain. The endocrine glands all work in concert, and when the ovaries begin shutting down, this places an extra strain on both the thyroid and adrenals.

Dr. Broda Barnes has written an excellent book called *Hypothyroidism; The Unsuspected Illness*. Dr. Barnes suggests that basal body temperature can be a way of assessing metabolic rate to make a diagnosis. Dr. Barnes suggests using desiccated thyroid if the resting body temperature is sub-normal to supply the thyroid gland with the essential building blocks to support its function. Most conventional doctors often wait until the thyroid is very weak and damaged before using replacement thyroid therapy. Then they are likely to use synthetic thyroid hormone.

In my opinion, desiccated thyroid, which consists of thyroxine as well as iodine, tyrosine and other building blocks of thyroid, best helps to rebuild the thyroid and improve its functioning.

However, the use of nutritional supplements should be the first line of attack for hypothyroidism. If this does not help, desiccated thyroid should be used, leaving synthetic thyroid as the last resort.

Nutritionally, these supplements are helpful:

• **Tyrosine, B6, zinc** and **kelp** to treat thyroid deficiency

• **Vitamin A** for the proper functioning of the pituitary gland, so it stimulates the thyroid to produce thyroxine. 10,000 I.U. per day should be sufficient, but any supplementation for thyroid problems must be arrived at with your doctor.

INCONTINENCE

Urinary incontinence is the involuntary loss of urine. It is often considered a consequence of aging, but this is not the case. Women seem more susceptible to this condition, probably because, in childbirth, their bladder sphincter muscles have weakened somewhat, or they may have pressure on the bladder from uterine prolapse. As they get older, men are also susceptible because the prostate at the base of the penis enlarges and puts pressure on the urethra, which causes frequent urination. There are many suggestions that can help this condition.

• First of all, avoid alcohol, which is a great irritant to the bladder sphincter.

• Avoid caffeine, which causes increased urination. Caffeine is not just in coffee—it's also found in cola beverages, chocolate, and many over-the-counter medications.

• Give up smoking, which also causes irritation of the bladder. Be aware that "smoker's cough" can cause bladder leakage when the body goes into reflex spasm from the cough.

• Maintain an optimum diet, which will help you lose excess weight; this itself will help take the pressure off the abdomen and the bladder to reduce incontinence. A high fiber diet will also ensure normal bowel movements and eliminate the pressure from constipation which can also irritate the bladder. The proper diet would be high in fiber, with enough fluid to keep the fiber from making you more constipated. It would include a lot of vegetables, moderate amounts of fruit, whole grains, nuts, seeds, legumes, fish and chicken.

Record everything you eat or drink, the times you urinate and the times you have incontinence. After a week or so, you may see a pattern—a relationship between what you eat and how often your bladder leaks. It may be a simple matter of drinking too much fluid. However, dehydrating yourself is not the answer to this condition.

The advice that urologists give for this condition includes what is called "double voiding." After you urinate, remain on the toilet and wait for any excess urine that remains to leave the bladder. You can apply gentle pressure over the pubic bone, or bend forward a bit to encourage all the urine to run out.

The exercises that are especially important for the bladder are well known, and are called Kegel exercises. Dr. Kegel felt that the bladder sphincter muscles, just like any other muscles, could be exercised and trained. His instructions are to pretend you're tightening the muscles around the anus and then pretend you're holding back the urine—this identifies the two groups of muscles that you're going to be working on. Then, starting at the anus, tighten the muscles and proceed forward, tightening the muscles at the urethra; hold this to a count of four, then release.

Dr. Kegel advised that this be done for two minutes three times a day, or at least a hundred times daily. You can do the Kegel exercises when you're waiting at a traffic light, reading this chapter, or waiting for a bus. They are simple, can be done anywhere and they are very helpful.

INSOMNIA

Menopausal complaints include several types of sleep disturbances including insomnia, early waking and excessive dreaming. Most women who are bothered by hot flushes at night complain of inability to return to sleep. Some women must change their drenched night clothes or bed linens before being able to return to sleep. The problem here is the hot flushes. When they are treated (see page 9) often the sleep disturbance goes away. However there are other ways to prevent insomnia:

• Avoid coffee or alcohol or a late dinner.

• Don't do strenuous exercise before bedtime (however intercourse often helps one sleep.)

- Take a hot bath with Epsom salts, baking soda or vinegar and play some quiet music.
- Play a relaxation tape while lying in bed.
- Exercise daily.
- Take vitamin E, 400 I.U., one to three at bedtime.
- Try one of the following herbal remedies:

- **Skullcap,** 10 to 15 drops in a few ounces of water
- **Hops, valerian** and **skullcap** mixture, one to two capsules at bedtime.
- **Women's Precious Pills** (Chinese herbs), 10 to 20 pellets before bedtime.
- The homeopathic remedy **Coffea** 6c, 4 drops, one to two doses at bedtime for an overactive mind.

OVERWEIGHT

There is some good news about women at menopause and weight gain. In the premenopausal period women have a tendency to gain 7 to 10 pounds, which seems to be an adaptive mechanism designed to keep the levels of estrogen up by increasing fat stores as the estrogen output decreases in the ovaries. Actually, after menopause is completed, this excess weight can be easily shed. Not realizing this, some women may get discouraged at this time, give up the struggle and let their weight escalate. It is essential to continue your exercise daily if you want to maintain a healthy weight.

A diet high in whole grains, vegetables, and beans and low in fat and sugar will help you to shed those extra pounds slowly and healthfully.

Obesity is common in our society, and there seems to be no easy answer or quick fix. Women need to explore both the emotional and physical reasons for being overweight. It is true that women are apt to gain weight at times of hormonal shifts such as adolescence, pregnancy and menopause, but there are many other reasons for overweight, which usually begins long before menopause.

To compound the problem, the birth control pill, estrogen

and progesterone all contribute to weight gain due to fluid retention and fat deposits. Estrogen, especially, causes localized fat deposits in the thighs, hips and breasts.

On the physical and nutritional side, often food allergies play a part in obesity. You may be eating foods the body considers allergenic, and this can lead to an excess amount of fluid retention. Therefore, food allergy testing may be helpful if you have "tried every diet in the book."

Small frequent meals are important for weight loss rather than starving through the day and making up for it with one large meal at night. Only a portion of this meal can be metabolized and utilized. The excess will go into fat storage.

Any diet must be undertaken gradually. Drink lots of water to flush out toxins and, above all, avoid constipation. Proper dieting is a form of detoxification.

VAGINAL DRYNESS AND VAGINITIS

The mucous membrane of the vagina has three layers. The most superficial layer is composed of thin cells that secrete mucus. These cells are matured by the presence of estrogen. With a relative lack of estrogen they thicken and lose their ability to produce lubricating mucus. The dryness that results can lead to minor abrasions from the friction of intercourse or even washing and wiping the genitals. These tiny tears can then allow for the introduction of an invasive organism, bacteria or yeast that can lead to an irritating infection.

The oral use of **black cohosh** as part of a menopausal supplement program can help correct vaginal dryness. Vitamin E can be used orally, 400 I.U.s once or twice a day. A capsule can also be inserted into the vagina to relieve dryness or vitamin E suppositories are available in health food stores.

Estrogen cream provides an excellent treatment for the drying vaginal lining, which is actually due to estrogen deficiency. Now women can also obtain what may be the safer estriol cream from various pharmacies on prescription. Estriol 0.5 mg/gram is the standard concentration and one-fourth of a teaspoon two or three times per week is usually sufficient to protect the vaginal lining. Depending on the severity of the case, some women may be advised to take a daily dose for a week or two at the start of treatment.

To prevent yeast vaginitis:

- Avoid tight synthetic undergarments and pants.
- Wear loose cotton underwear, which may have to be boiled or ironed to kill all the yeast spores.
- Avoid acidifying spermicides which can irritate the vagina and encourage yeast overgrowth.
- Don't use scented or dyed toilet paper, pads or tampons.
- If you are still menstruating make sure the tampons themselves are not the cause of your symptoms. Alternate between pads and tampons. Today there is a pad on the market that uses sphagnam moss as its absorbent. The pads are thin and comfortable, and the moss controls odor.
- Have your partner use a condom to avoid passing yeast back to you during intercourse.
- Use natural douches such as **baking soda** or vinegar (one tablespoon in a pint of water); **acidophilus** or **yogurt; boric acid** (one teaspoon in a pint of water.)

Treatment for yeast vaginitis is often by douche. In some cases this may be enough to provide symptomatic relief. However, if the condition is persistent, it must be treated on a broader scale with diet, acidophilus by mouth, acidophilus mixed with yogurt and applied vaginally and sometimes oral antifungal medications. For more information please read about candidiasis, page 9.

Acupuncturists report considerable success in the treatment of both hot flashes and atrophic vaginitis. The herbal and homeopathic treatments for menopause are also important for a healthy vagina.

RESOURCES for Natural Hormone Alternatives

Progesterone cream is available in health food stores and natural estrogen cream is becoming more available without prescription. Oral forms of natural progesterone and estrogen are available on prescription from many pharmacies including the following:

Delk Pharmacy, Columbia, TN. 615-388-3952.

Women's International Pharmacy, Madison, WI. 800-279-5708.

Professional & Technical Services, Inc., Portland, OR. 800-648-8211.

BIBLIOGRAPHY

Abraham, Guy E., MD, *Physician Information Manual*. 1993. Optimox Corporation, PO Box 3378, Torrance, CA 90510-3378.

Andrews, Lynn, *Women at the Edge of Two Worlds*. HarperCollins, New York, 1993.

Atkins, Robert, MD, *Dr. Atkins' Health Revolution*. Houghton Mifflin Company, 1989.

Coney, Sandra, *The Menopause Industry: How the Medical Establishment Exploits Women*. Hunter House, 1994.

Crook, William, MD, *The Yeast Connection*. Professional Books, Inc., Jackson, TN, 1983.

Follingstad, A. H. "Estriol, the Forgotten Estrogen?" *Journal of the American Medical Association*, 239:1978.

Gaby, Alan R., MD, *Preventing and Reversing Osteoporosis*. Prima Publishing, 1993.

Kamen, Betty, *Hormone Replacement Therapy: Yes or No?* Nutrition Encounter, Inc., 1993.

Lee, John R., MD, *Natural Progesterone-The Multiple Roles of a Remarkable Hormone*. BLL Publishing, P.O. Box 2068, Sebastopol, CA 95473.

Weed, Susun, S., *Menopausal Years: The Wise Woman Way*. Ash Tree Publishing, Woodstock, New York, 1992.